THE CLOUDS ARE MADE OF PAPER HEARTS

Peter Townsend

The Clouds are made of Paper Hearts

Copyright © 2023 by Peter Townsend

For information contact :

othrart.com

Book and Cover design by Peter Townsend & Onur Media

ISBN: 979-8-218-13078-7

First Edition : January 2023

T h e   c l o u d s   a r e   m a d e   o f   p a p e r
h e a r t s

To a field of sunflowers

CONTENTS

Looking for somewhere to go

When my dreams are gone

Somewhere inside my mind

My dreams live on

Or someone to make a choice

On these things unknown

I never had a dream at all

- illusions

Nothing ever changes

My love for you has spaces

- love outlet

I don't believe in stars

I don't believe in night

I know the moon only shines

Because the sun gives it light

- sun

T h e   c l o u d s   a r e   m a d e   o f   p a p e r
h e a r t s

In between these different lovers

I found you with another

In-between my vows

I saw you dancing on the clouds

And between now and forever

You're still the only one around

- *where were you*

This empty void inside your heart

A blur of pain and love collide

I gave a pathway out

When I got lost inside your eyes

Now I'm the void between your chest

And you fight to get me out

I'll turn your pain back into love

You just have to hear me out

- listen please

T h e   c l o u d s   a r e   m a d e   o f   p a p e r
h e a r t s

How dreadful this world would be

If I had to go thru, without you

- *this time*

I was aware

That eventually you'll forget

the things I'll always remember

- *last week*

Honestly, If I marry and it's not you

I'll still love you more than her

- 4 am thought

I hear voices in my heart

They only talk about you

- *voices*

I hear voices in my heart

They only talk about you

T h e   c l o u d s   a r e   m a d e   o f   p a p e r
h e a r t s

I miss you,

First three words I've written since

Last seeing you wave goodbye

You told me nothings ending

So, this tragedy is mine

- *imysm*

I could write an epic

All about your presence

When I met you

It was your smile that

That left me breathless

So now I toil over seconds

Trying to find the words

To describe perfection.

- *this real life*

The clouds are made of paper
hearts

Every word you said to me

Plays like madness in my head

- *Plot twist*

The clouds are made of paper hearts

This feeling of being wanted,

Is the closest my mortal body has felt
eternal

- *for a long time*

Odd,

I don't remember how I met you

It feels like all the memories I have of past

Include you in them

These places I have been

Only feel your presence

Like you merged in every second

Not a single moment were we strangers

Bound together somehow, we are the same

Pulling on a string

When you're away

I feel your distance, I hear your pain

I know when you are looking a thousand
miles away

- I know you

I know you don't love me yet

But this is enough for me, anyway.

- *bliss*

I promised I would stop feeling for you

But, even when I'm empty

You are my nothing

- all the way

I'm looking for your heart

On this winding autumn road

Music echoes between

the whispers of your voice

And each turn as we approach

I can feel your subtle grasp

Even though you never move

I feel you hold my hand

- *countryside*

It feels like every other moment

That we've had thus far

Like seconds pass on the front

Now the past is gone

The blur of your love

I must admit

Has become a little too hard

- blur

How is it that a picture is perfect

A picture worth a thousand

Doesn't matter how you word it

- *a thousand words*

I really love this album

When I heard it in your car

So, I purchased it on vinyl

But I placed it on the wall

I can't listen to those lyrics

It's not the same when you are gone

- gone

One day these feelings will fade

A little spark without a flame

- *fireplace*

These feelings deep inside

Thinking I can never grow

Every time I see the future

I never see myself

- *tunnel vision*

I would cross the oceans

And trek thru all the seas

Just to find your love

Inside a package so clean

And even though it's obvious

Everywhere we go

There isn't anyone else

I'd rather call home

- our love

I stare at the uneven lines

Across the bumpy painted surface

And as the hours passed

Id question if it was worth it

You called me out the blue

For no reason, just because you wanted to

I no longer wonder what it's worth

When everything is you

- *everything is you*

Tell me that you love me

Moments happen everyday

Our time together months ago

Felt like yesterday

I'm in a rush to a forever

You said, take your time with me

Somehow that sounded like a never

Wish you were in love with me

- downfall of a dreamer

If everything was alright

Would your love

be walking around my mind

playing like a song

nightmares or lullabies?

- *I just woke up*

I must remember I'm made of clay

So, when it rains

I fall away

- *I'm just a man*

September comes and goes

And these memories of you haunt me

when there's nothing left to do

- *gram*

the sun was perfect

when it fell away

the sky was purple

with shades of grey

and all your words

are on my mind

asked if it could fade away

your agony and daily pain

tears in your eyes

you can barely see

with pastoral breath

I calmy say

That there is nowhere I'd rather be

than in this time

where I know you

so, if you leave, I go too

- *lights out*

I can feel you drifting

Away from me

The Seasons are changing

And so are we

Like ice my love kept you

Close to my heart

But the sun has come

We're starting to melt apart

It's getting thinner

Each day that passes by

The spring flower's blossoms

But our love is about to die

- *there's something on the trees*

New pages

Inside of books

Barely written

Tales of lovers

Are bound to each other

- I wrote about you

I took my time

Trying to find

A new way to you

You don't believe

I'd stay here

And wait for you

I think

Some things are meant to be

We'll plant our seeds

Pray time and rain

Grows our little tree

- cedar oaks

I think you

Started to fall for me too

Before I said I love her

I only meant you

- *shades of you*

If I told a story about love

I'd write myself a parachute above

Keep it nestled with the birds

Just in case things fall apart

I am starting to realize

These clouds are made of paper hearts

- safety net

You

Are like

A slice of paradise

And I am the shadow of a man

left on one knee to never stand

and it hurts to say

that it works this way

when there's no wedding dress

to throw away

- no oaths

T h e   c l o u d s   a r e   m a d e   o f   p a p e r
h e a r t s

I thought I could send you letters

Just to tell you who I am

Detailing all the reasons

Why I could be your man

Elaborating about you

Things you've heard all before

You were never that romantic

So, you can never see me more

- letters

You were born today,

And I'll tell you how

The ground of the earth opened

And started to sprout

The waters fell

And filled an empty surface

Forming oceans and making islands

It was all done on purpose

- *creation*

The clouds are made of paper hearts

Every night I see you

When the day light turns to black

Each time like a forever

Our adventures never end

You always say the same

When the sunlight starts to break

Thru my eyelids I awaken

You say you'll never fade.

- I only see you in my dreams

T h e   c l o u d s   a r e   m a d e   o f   p a p e r
h e a r t s

It feels like I'm bursting at my seams

you're my everything

I called when it's too late

For me to say that everything's ok

- *later*

These winding streets

I drive thru at midnight

Eyes on the road

You sing till daylight

We talk about the rolling hills

Lights in the distance

that don't seem real

you laugh at jokes I know aren't funny

I roll my window down to see what's
coming

The chill is mixed with evergreen air

I look back inside

Straining my eyes to see

Its breaks my heart

You're no longer in my passenger seat

- *I hear your shadows*

The clouds are made of paper
hearts

Our loves departed

And I don't think you can claim

That I'm the one that started

I guess everything can change

I tossed every souvenir you left behind

I can't remember better times

So now I'm fading please

Let me find a better life

- separation

You've been broken so deeply

No matter how much they love

It all ends up the same

At the bottom of this endless well

- *drowning*

Your skin

Smells like

The thoughts I can't explain

In the distant corners of my brain

That fall into my hands like tears

When I remember you're just a dream.

- aroma

In all chaos I ache for what never will.

Unsure if the shock of you

Was worth the pain I felt.

You lay there neatly nestled

Between a meadow and forest felling
leaves

So distant from my glare

Yet deep inside of me

I will love you forever

So, I mourn something I never had

- unrequited

Aisle by aisle making sure every item is
accounted

Heading towards the checkout counter

I rummage thru my pockets

Looking for my card so can pay for all my
items

you come up behind me

And ask

"Did you check our grocery list"

- *next earth*

My mind is so forgetful

I must attach our moments on to feelings

Just so I remember

So, when I say that I miss you

It means more than just that instant

Its everything you are

Every second

Every minute

- I forgot you

I wonder if with your friends

You talk about our conversations

Do you whisper our adventures

To anyone who will listen

Does your closet persons know

Whether or not you ever miss me

I really wish I knew what you were
thinking

- conversations

Searching for a way to express these
thoughts

without words to give them definition

only I can feel them in this body

even if it rots

This feeling lingers in my cells

How can I explain something

Even I don't know that well

I can hear my bones screaming

For answer I can't give

It's crazy I have so much life left to live

- 30 years asleep

why am I blue

can you see my hue?

I had everything working in my favor

So why am I blue.

- *blue*

These pastel tears

Don't wash away

They fall

And stain your face

- *pastel tears*

we were like robots

Storing endless memories

55

- *hard drive*

I'm sorry

I wrote this when broken

These feelings an ocean

Its sinking this boat and

I'm floating

But my energy's low

When I can't see where I'm going

- *down*

Pardon my thoughts

They are all from the heart

It derives from my brain

And that tears me apart

Hurts when I'm here

So inside I'm all gone

I know No one is alone

If you look at the sky

We all have his love.

- hope

I hear your words as I read each letter

- *9 words*

Today you told me about him

Detailing all your feelings

A lot like mine for you

inside I scream

But outside I hold your hand

The only thing that I can do

- silent

I understand

The complex hymns the birds are singing

It's your favorite tune

I know every word

I had a dream about you

- I reject this idea

When we are on the phone

I can see the creases in your face

Spaces like a path

Between your places

- *details*

With eyes like those

What does it take to know

I feel like I know you well

I wish you knew yourself

- *Oh wow*

The crowded air of the airport lobby

Seconds before seeing you finally

- first encounters

Do you remember when I held your hand

Seated on frozen seats before our train

Pulling you closer to block wind behind

And Staring at your Redding skin

What a beautiful design

I memorized the textures of your palm

Perfect I thought

But my memory is flawed

When I grabbed your hand, you froze

Unsure of where'd it go

Your past flashed up like a storm

Shivering down your bones

As I pulled you closer you feared me

More and more

When it all ended you smiled and sighed

One that I heard and thought

Everything was fine

- *trauma*

we connect on every level

when I think of you

I forget where I end

But we both have so much trauma

I hope we aren't a trauma bonding

all I see is you forever

No matter how much I deny it

- trauma bond

The clouds are made of paper
hearts

where were you

when I met her

standing right beside her

I couldn't see you at the time

but that doesn't make it better

- *impossibilities*

The clouds are made of paper
hearts

every night I dream of you

just reflections of my memories

- memories

How long can I hold back

These words pounding in my chest

- *I love you*

You are always told that you're perfect

Yet you never feel worth it

So, do I tell you you're endless?

Or let you sink in your curses

I'm sorry I love you right now

I know you only want him

So, I'll keep it inside

Because today you need your friend.

- just friends

I'm worried about
having so many things to say
to you
that all the words in the world
wouldn't be able to express them
there are a lot of ways
to go about arranging things
I want to do it extravagantly
show, not tell, you
how you light up my sky
or something romantic like that
but in simple terms
I just want you to know that I care

- in simple terms

the panels on the floor are laughing
squeaking, every other step containing
some wonderful memory
the walls give a big, knowing smile
holding in late-night stories and secrets
shared over the phone
so secure and so comforting
but the wallpaper peels a little, revealing
fluttering feelings
nervous yet sure, gentle glances here and
there
for, so sweetly, friendship has built a
house for love
and the fireplace lets out a sigh of relief
warmth, warmth, take it all, it breathes
open the windows, let the light in, let the
whole world know

- house

I think, maybe, I saw you once–
yes, I know that's impossible,
but I think, maybe, I did–
in the grocery store
grabbing a box of my favorite cereal
on tiptoes to reach the highest shelf
or at that park I'd pass by
resting under the shade of an ancient tree
with a cup of coffee in your hand
because the first time we spoke
felt like coming back to a piece of home
something that had been with me all this
time
the joy in that moment screamed,
"hey! how lovely to run into you again!"
you made your way in to my life, then–
not in the grocery store aisle, but
everything about you was so familiar and
right
that I couldn't believe I'd only just made
your acquaintance

- grocery store

a fresh coat of paint on a long-lived wall
two children helping up another from a
fall
three words that speak more than enough
four arms embracing when life gets tough
five seconds more of sweet, golden sun
six beautiful things– you're my favorite
one

- beautiful things

if the wind would allow it, I'd take it like a
train to you
floating like it's a regular pastime, make
myself miniscule
fit in with the orange-brown leaves on
journeys of their own
do you think every drifting leaf is a
resolute lover, too?
for, if not in love, into what have they
fallen?
I'd wonder about things like this along the
way
until I made it to your doorstep, all autumn
and enchantment

- visits in November

standing under the night with you
and the sky is such a royal blue
there's not very much to say
so let's just stand in the quiet.
wind in your hair, cold but inviting
and the power lines hum a lullaby
there are two different kinds of electric:
one, you feel in a crowded, noisy room
abuzz with excitement and thrill
and another, you feel at 3 in the morning
in the sting of the outside air, an angel by
your side
I'll let you in on this: I prefer the latter

- electric

heard a tune on the street the other day
couldn't see where it was coming from
didn't think much of it then, but now that I
do
it sort of reminds me a bit of me and you
not that the melody poured out how I feel
when I talk with you for hours on the
phone
and not that the lyrics spoke all that I'd
say
if my feelings could be expressed in words
alone
it was more the fact that my eyes couldn't
place
the music, or that my steps could not
retrace
to it, and that, nevertheless, I still felt the
presence
of the notes drifting joyously along
so, even as I do not see you each day,
being that we are quite far away,
I think you get it– the tune still rings on

- street music

found in a bed of dry grass, on the floor
edges slightly torn and cracked once
before
I hand over an orange maple leaf to you
you reach in your pocket for one for me,
too
bruised and battered, but marvelous still
if the last thing I do is protect it, I will
pressed snugly in between crisp, white
pages
adorned with illustrations of magic and
mages
prolonged under their warm and seasonal
spell
remembering the autumn in which it first
fell
not any more soles to step down on its
glow
not any more souls to abuse what they
know
safe on the shelf and surrounded by love
such preserving your heart is the thing I
dream of

- maple leaf

when there are mountains to climb
and you look down at an abyss below
just know I'll be a rock for you to grab
onto
I'm not going anywhere– steady,
unmoving
and I know you can get yourself over the
hill
but if you need it, I'll be your leg up

- *leg up*

little dove outside the window
let me mend your broken wing
I understand you're tired and hurt
but you've got this resilient spring
and I know that we, together,
can get through most anything
so we'll go on, hand in hand–
or, should I say, wing in wing

- wing in wing

The clouds are made of paper
hearts

it's laundry day
and I'm looking at this sweater that
reminds me of yours
I remember the day you wore it, out on an
adventure
and I'm smiling, grinning ear to ear
thinking about the handful of stories in the
pockets
the moments that must've woven
themselves in with the yarn
please keep it forever, if you can–
yesterday looks a blessing on you

- sweater

if I could describe you...
well, I'll describe you.
not a particularly tricky affair
except that it is–
for you can't be contained
in a few lines about
your soft, shoulder length hair
but I'll try anyway
to capture how your eyes shine
from behind the frames of your glasses
how, with a breathtaking smile,
you brighten my day
and do the same for
any and everyone who passes
but what I'm saying is that
I can't paint a picture
of exactly the way you look
because your heart is inside
and it'd be a shame
if its beauty
was wholly left out of the book

- picture

like a butterfly upon becoming a
butterfly–
breaking loose of its bounds
stretching and flitting about
as if delighted to see the sun again after a
long slumber
as if to say, "why, I never considered
how lovely the world might look
from all the way up here!"
a vibrant dash across the sky
striking and powerful, yet gentle as can be
curiosity overpowering shakiness
eagerness to explore everything
I feel this way when I look at you
well, I suppose, after all
that's why they call it "butterflies"

- butterflies

looking back, I don't remember
knowing you'd show up when you did
but some part of me must have
really been anticipating your arrival
because when we found each other
you didn't need the key under the rug–
you already had one of your own

- key

can you recognize your favorite star?
because I think, no matter where you are
mine would still be you– near or far
each night I'd love you even more
whether the fog covers up your bright
or you're shining vividly, on a clear night
I'll always be here, adoring the sight
treasuring you with all my might

- *unconditional*

the warm water on your skin

reminds you of different things

you cannot remember a single word

just tall grass and humid wind

you found a keychain he gave you once

hidden in that box under your bed

the moments blurry and somewhat boring

you left his love at summers end

- seasonal affection

you grew tired of me

I can tell our sun is setting

Now I lay beside

Someone I do not recognize

You wanted to see the world

But we became trapped

in this place that we reside

now every time we say goodnight

it's from our own separate sides

- strange lovers

so many times, I sat beside

you in hospital rooms

the frigid air and endless loops

of precarious beeps the perfect tune

if you listen closely between the sounds

you hear the prayers from all around

as some are healed, and others drown

there's no comfort in the waiting rooms

just hopeful faces, and morbid frowns

so, I never shared my point of view

if it ever seemed like I didn't care

it's because I cared too much for you

to let this darkness come around

knowing these could be your last

your family tree grows more with me

so, I promise you'll see us all again

- sick

The clouds are made of paper hearts

I remember when you would hold me

I remember when you would tell me

I remember when you would show me

I remember when you would help me

I remember when you would love me

I remember when you would scold me

I remember when you would teach me

I remember when you would

I remember what you said

- I forgot